The Basic Essentials of
MOUNTAIN BIKING

by Michael A. Strassman

**Illustrations by
John McMullen**

ICS BOOKS, Inc.
Merrillville, Indiana

THE BASIC ESSENTIALS OF MOUNTAIN BIKING

Printed in U.S.A.

Published by:
ICS Books, Inc.
One Tower Plaza
107 E. 89th Avenue
Merrillville, IN 46410

ACKNOWLEDGEMENTS
To Judy Strassman and Steve York who helped write the chapters on maintenance and showed me their secret rides along the Salmon River.

DEDICATION
This book is dedicated to the dead-end gang.

Library of Congress Cataloging-in-Publication Data

Strassman, Michael A.
    Mountain biking: the basic essentials of / by Michael Strassman ; illustrations by John McMullen.
        p.   cm. -- (The Basic essentials series)
    ISBN 0-934802-47-5
    1. All terrain bicycles.   I. Title
GV1056.S77   1989
796.6--dc20
                                                    89-37910
                                                        CIP

TABLE OF CONTENTS

Figure 1

1. THE MOUNTAIN BIKE

Yesterday, I rode my bike up a mountain. It did not take a lot of effort. I was only gone for a couple of hours. An easy trail, it gently rises up an ancient glacial moraine. Lanky pines shade the way past granite boulders and aspen trees. As I pedaled, I marveled at this machine, this tool.

The mountain bike combines the stalwart engineering of the motorcycle with the refined craftsmanship of the racing bike. It is one of the most efficient self-propelled instruments ever invented.

The surface of the trail is compact dirt. My wide tires bite firmly. By summer's end, this trail will be soft from hooves and boots. A mountain biker's nightmare. I will shift to my lowest gears and plow through it. For now, my effort is easy and rhythmic. I have become part of this forest.

The wildlands can present their own surprises. Boulders, remnants of a recent avalanche, have fallen across the trail. Their sharp corners could puncture a tire, or flatten a rim. Confidently, I pull my front wheel upon them, pedal hard, slamming my rear tire against the rock. The wheel rises over the obstacle, grabs the firm soil and propels me onward.

1

Should I get into trouble, I am my own savior. I carry all tools, all knowledge. A broken chain can be repaired, preventing a long walk out. A sudden storm will not make my ride uncomfortable. Even now, I cross a thin layer of snow, vestige of a recent tempest. My bicycle handles expertly through this new medium.

Finally, cresting the moraine, I enter a fairyland of white rimmed pines. I slip on the snow, regain my straight line and pedal towards the lake. The clouds have broken to reveal banners of gold light falling on frosted mountains. I pause at the scene, lower my seat, and descend.

* * * *

The mountain bike has brought me to many wonderful places. Places I never could have gone to on my old ten speed. The skinny tires would not grip the trail, the thin rims would crumble upon the rocks. Mountain bikes give you the freedom to ride almost anywhere in any conditions. Your mountain bike can take you through snow, across streams, down old railroad grades and into the back country. They are perfect for negotiating the rough terrain of the city. The mountain bike opens up a whole new world.

The majority of bicycles purchased today are mountain bikes. Their versatility and comfort have made them popular. When you first look at a mountain bike you will notice several differences from your standard ten speeds. The tires are the most obvious. Wide and knobby, these fat monsters provide better traction, shock absorption, and stability. They are more resistant to puncture and far more durable than skinny tires. So, mountain bikes are often called "fat tire bikes" when compared to their delicate ten speed cousins.

Many recreational cyclists complain about the hunched-over, wind resistant posture of racing bikes. On the mountain bike, you sit upright. Unlike the drop-style handlebars of racing bikes, the wide handlebars are designed for maneuverability and handling. All your controls are mounted here; the brakes are close to the hand grips, next to them are the shift levers. Stopping, shifting and steering are all within finger's reach.

Mountain bikes provide a wide range of gearing to make riding over varied terrain easier. Generally, mountain bikes are geared lower than road bikes. Most have anywhere from fifteen to twenty-one speeds: five to seven sprockets on the rear and three chain rings on the front. The smallest chain ring is for ascending, the middle chain ring is for the flats, and the large chain ring is for descents. Mix and match them as you please!

The brakes are perhaps the most important component of any bicycle. The mountain bike's brakes are designed for durability and function in wet and muddy conditions. Get to know your brakes and how they work. An unsafe brake is an unsafe bike.

The heart of the bike is the frame. At first glance, the mountain bike frame does not appear to be any different from other bikes. However, the uses and abuses of the mountain bike demand a sturdy, but lightweight construction. Most mountain bikes use chrome-moly or aluminum, although such space age materials as kevlar, carbon fiber and titanium are also being used. Frames tend to have compact geometries for better handling, greater clearance for obstacles and a lightweight but strong composition for durability and efficiency.

Most important, mountain bikes are designed for fun. Ride anywhere, on all terrain, in any conditions. Relax in stability and comfort, or push yourself up a steep hill. Remember, these machines take skill to operate and demand self-sufficiency on the part of the rider. An accident or breakdown could happen far from any help. But, by knowing how your bike works, we avoid breakdowns; by concentrating on developing riding skills, we avoid accidents. Let's learn how it's done. Build your confidence and have more fun.

2. CHOOSING A MOUNTAIN BIKE

When choosing a mountain bike there are several things you must consider. Decide what your primary use of the bike will be. Will you be commuting? Racing? Fitness riding? Maybe you just want to get out and play. Consider where you intend to ride. Maybe you want to ride trails in the back country, or perhaps just run down to the store for a dozen eggs. Price is another consideration. What are you willing to spend in exchange for quality and function? These are the kinds of questions you must ask yourself before you walk into a bike shop.

Price

Quality mountain bikes range in price from $250.00 for an around town bike to $5,000.00 for a custom made carbon fiber racing bike. Lower prices mean a less durable, more basic mountain bike. Mid-range priced bikes ($350.00 to $600.00) give you your best value for the money. These are sturdy bikes that hold up to abuse, but won't abuse your wallet. Higher priced bikes ($700.00 to $5,000.00) are designed for the serious enthusiasts and racers.

These have exotic frame materials and highly refined component designs. They offer the best performance of any mountain bike.

After considering your budget, ask yourself what you intend to do with a mountain bike. There are many different types of mountain bikes for a variety of needs. There are cruisers, cross-bikes, racing bikes, BMX bikes, and trials bikes. All of these can be used in the dirt, yet some are better for different applications.

Figure 2
Cruiser

Cruisers

If you intend to commute short distances, or anticipate light, recreational riding, you won't need a wide range of gearing or heavy duty off-road equipment. Instead, consider an around-town bike. Gaining in popularity is the "beach cruiser." This is a mid-weight bike with upright handle bars, one to five speeds, and a very comfortable, relaxed ride. These bikes resemble the old Schwinn cruiser frame; coaster brakes, fat white-wall tires, and a basket on the front.

Figure 3
Cross-bike

Cross-Bikes

If you expect to do your around town riding quickly and efficiently you may want a lightweight, multi-speed, hybrid mountain
bike or cross-bike. These bikes are a cross between the efficiency
of a road bike and the handling of a mountain bike. Designed with
a geometry similar to road bikes, hybrids share many of the same
components as true mountain bikes. Tires are fatter than a road
bike yet thinner than a true mountain bike. There is a wide range
of gearing. Cross-bikes also have two different styles of handlebars.
One is a flat or upright bar mounted with thumb shifters and brake
levers by the grip. The other is a traditional ten-speed style bar
with the shift levers mounted on the end of the curved grip. Whether
you have the flat bar or the curved depends on how you intend to
ride the bike. The cross-bike is an excellent choice for city dwellers
who rarely take their bike in the dirt.

Figure 4
Trial Bike

Trials Bikes

Trials bikes are another type of competitive bike that are designed to be jumped, hopped, and maneuvered over obstacles. The goal of trials is to perform these feats without your feet touching the ground. Originally an event designed for motorcycles, trials have become a fascinating spectator sport for mountain bike competition. Trials bike frames tend to be smaller than the standard mountain bike design. They are also reinforced to avoid frame flexing which enhances maneuverability. The tires have almost no air pressure for maximum traction. Trials is quite unlike mountain biking. It is a competition you must see to believe.

Figure 5
A Mountain Touring Bike loaded down.

The Mountain Touring Bike

Similar to the recreational mountain bike is the mountain touring bike. Although designed for carrying loads in the backcountry,
this bike is often seen touring on the road with skinnier tires. While
the touring bike will take you anywhere that recreational bikes will,
it has a more relaxed frame geometry (longer frame angles) suited
for carrying loads such as touring gear. On the frame are three sets
of studs for water bottle cages. Mounted on the front and rear are
racks for carrying gear. There is no difference in gearing and componentry between this bike and the recreational bike.

Figure 6
The classic mountain bike.

The Classic Mountain Bike

This is the kind of bike most people think of when they hear the words "mountain bike." Designed to be used on rough roads, back country trails and/or challenging terrain, mountain bikes fall into several categories. There are recreational mountain bikes, racing bikes, specialized mountain bikes, and mountain touring bikes.

Recreational mountain bikes are designed for riding on dirt roads, through streams, over rock, and along trails. One of the more popular styles today, recreational mountain bikes provide a comfortable, stable ride in a variety of riding situations. With 18 speeds at your finger tips, you'll find these bikes are versatile in any terrain. A longer frame geometry combined with stability in steering makes it a more predictable riding bike.

Racing Mountain Bikes

Racing mountain bikes are designed for durability, efficiency, and high speed maneuverability. Frames are constructed of lightweight alloy steel or aluminum. A tighter frame geometry places your weight farther back over the rear wheel to increase traction on hills. A steeper head tube angle provides quicker, more precise handling. Componentry is built to perform smoothly in the worst environments and the most demanding situations. Because racing bikes are on the cutting edge of mountain bike technology, what you see on a racing bike today may become standard equipment for your recreational bike tomorrow.

BMX

BMX bikes are those little trick bikes you see the neighborhood kids showing off with all the time. But don't shrug these cycles off as toys. There are six year olds that can out- perform their big brothers on any vacant lot. BMX is an acronym for bicycle moto-cross, and were the first popular bikes to be ridden in the dirt. The latest rage is the freestyle BMX bike. Outfitted with features like framestands, axle pegs and slick tires, these bikes allow riders to perform gymnastic feats never imagined on a bicycle ten years ago.

The best bike for you is a matter of personal preference. Just don't limit yourself by buying a bike that is specific to one aspect of mountain biking. The joys of mountain biking come from a variety of experiences, be it racing, touring or recreational riding. Ask around. Especially glean the advice of your bike shop; they will be up to date on the latest advances. Whatever you decide, be sure that you buy a bike that's comfortable and fun to ride.

3. RIDING SKILLS

We all know how to ride a bike. The mountain bike is not any different until we get into the dirt. But before we go racing down any Kamikaze downhills, let's learn a few of the basics on the flats.

Weight Shifts

Mountain bikes are remarkably stable. It doesn't take much effort to turn them. You'll notice that you can turn a mountain bike simply by shifting your weight and leaning slightly into the turn. This is important. Use your weight shift to initiate and hold turns. Use the handlebars for more precise movements. In a large sweeping turn, you can actually move the bike in the opposite direction of the turn while at the same time holding the bike in a lean. This quality enables the rider to steer around small obstacles in a high speed curve. It is the increased stability from the wide tire that allows you to do this.

Forward and rear weight shifts are important elements in mountain biking. There will be times when you will want to put more traction on the rear tire, or push your weight forward to clear an obstacle. Take the bike to an area of slippery traction and try standing up off the seat and pedaling. The rear tire will spin-out in the dirt. Now sit on the seat and watch how much more traction you get. On road bikes, we are used to standing up in the saddle in order to give the bike more power. But on mountain bikes, especially on hills, it is important to sit down. This requirement tends to work different muscles than a road bike does. It pumps your quads, instead of your calves.

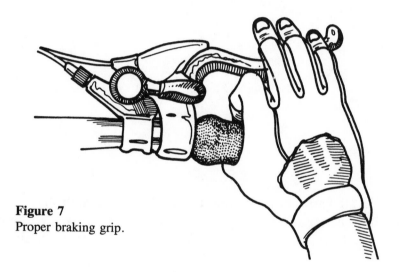

Figure 7
Proper braking grip.

Braking

Stopping the bike safely is important. Always pull on the rear brake before pulling on the front. Pulling on the front brake quickly will send you right over the handlebars. Try easing in on the rear brake and then squeezing the front brake tight as you stop.

Get to know what it takes to slow your bike down. Try coming to a dead stop at different speeds. When you get out in the woods, this knowledge will save you from an ugly collision with a rock or a log. It will also allow you to negotiate obstacles better. A lot of off-road skills combine speed with ability. Knowing how to slow your bike down to that perfect speed will help you out.

Turning

When going into a turn, slow down before the turn. There is nothing more frightening than realizing that you have entered a turn too fast. Turns often contain loose dirt and debris that can make the bike really squirrelly as you decelerate. Pulling hard on the rear brake will skid out the rear tire, and pulling hard on both brakes might send you over the handlebars. Keep your speed down as you enter a turn. Lean around the turn smoothly, avoiding obstacles. If you are going too fast, try and keep the bike in a straight line as you bring the bike to a halt. Don't try to blast through the turn, hoping that you'll make it. Stop. It'll save you from a meal of dirt.

Figure 8
Skid turn.

Skidding

Take the bike out into the dirt and practice skidding the rear wheel. Knowing how your bike responds in a skid may save you from a nasty fall. Start out slowly. Yank on the rear brake and throw your weight into the opposite direction of the turn, coming to a stop each time. Balance slightly with your inside foot, resting on it when you stop.

Once you've got the hang of it, instead of coming to a stop, try skidding and pedaling. (Perfect this technique until it becomes one smooth motion.) This is the skid turn, and will really help you on curvy descents, especially in soft sand.

The classic mountain bike image is of a rider skidding into a turn with their foot straight out touching the ground. Although this may be done on motorcycles, it is considered bad form on mountain bikes. Style-wise, expert riders feel a person should be able to control the mountain bike through proper lean and braking. The foot becomes a crutch, ready to help you out as you become off-balance. From a safety standpoint, that dangling foot could become caught on a branch or a rock and yank you off the bike, or worse, yank your foot into a sprain. However, in slow-speed maneuvering, a quick dab with the foot is O.K. It can save you from falling over.

Balance

Have you ever tried to balance a bicycle while it was standing still? This is a very difficult technique to master, but is definitely worth practicing. Often, you will have to balance the bike while travelling at slow speeds. Areas of slippery traction, steep sandy uphills and intricate obstacles all require keen balance and handling. Although some expert trials riders seem to be able to balance their bikes endlessly without movement, a little movement will be required for you to try it.

Cruise at a slow speed and use both brakes to bring you to a snail's pace. Dab the feet to keep you upright, then try balancing without using the feet at all. Now, as you lose momentum and start to feel out of balance, give a little power to the pedals, and brake. If you feel as if you are going to fall over, turn the front wheel in the direction you feel off-balance. It will keep you upright. Do it again. Try to practice minimizing those front wheel movements until you can balance. You are now creeping along far slower than you could ever pedal, but still keeping in balance.

Now work on expanding the idea. Put some rocks out in a tight slalom course in front of the bike. Now creep up and try maneuvering around them without falling over. (If you have toe

clips on your bike, be sure you are out of them for this one.) After
a while, you will get quite proficient at slow-speed maneuvering.

As the conditions worsen, you will want to add a wheelie or
actual hopping into your slow speed maneuvering. The wheelie
(pulling the front wheel into the air) will help you shift the balance
point (instead of simply turning the handlebars) as the front wheel
comes down on the unbalanced side. Don't pull the wheel up really
high; just a slight pull as you feel the bike begin to slow. This
technique is especially important in sandy terrain.

Figure 9
Hopping over a boulder.

Hopping

Hopping is a technique used by trials riders and free-style
riders. It involves bringing your bike to a stop and bringing both
wheels off the ground almost simultaneously.

It is done by clinching the brakes, bringing the bike to a stop and pulling the front wheel up in a wheelie. At the exact moment the front wheel has reached its zenith, the back brake is released and power is applied while abruptly pushing your weight forward. The rear tire leaves the ground and the bike is momentarily airborne.

Hopping is quite difficult to master on a conventional mountain bike, and is more suited for BMX, trials and free-style bikes. However, variations on the theme will help you in rocky terrain. A more detailed explanation will follow in the obstacles section.

Gearing

Mountain bikes usually have 15 to 27 gears to work with. Practice shifting and getting used to the amount of time it takes to shift into different gears, especially when shifting the front derailleur. There is a lot of space between those rings and it takes a lot longer for the gears to engage than on a tightly sprocketed racing bike. Gearing familiarity is important so that you may anticipate gear shifts before you get to the point you need them.

Let's say you are pedaling at a medium speed with the chain in the middle ring up front, and your highest gear in back. You see a hill approaching, gentle at the bottom, but steep at the top. You start up the hill and begin to shift the rear derailleur into the high gear. The chain clangs and jumps around as you try to apply more power against the shifting gear. Finally, the noise has ceased as you get the chain into the chosen gear. But it's not enough. The hill has steepened, and you need to be in the smallest front chain ring. So you shift again. You're trying to keep the speed up by applying more power, but the crazy thing won't shift. It's just rubbing against the front derailleur making an awful noise. All your friends are passing you, cranking away in their highest gears. Finally the bike slows down, and it shifts. You come to a stop and fall down in utter exhaustion.

Mountain bikes have a hard time shifting when a lot of force is being applied to the system. They need to jump large gaps, and a lot of tension on the chain bogs them down. By anticipating your gear shifts, you can shift before the force is required. That way the chain is in the proper gear when you need it.

Figure 10
Hyper-glide free wheel.

A recent development in mountain bike technology has helped to eliminate this problem. Small scallops are stamped onto the cogs that help guide the chain from one gear to the next. This is called Hyper-glide and helps the bike shift under power. However, the problem is not totally eliminated. You still must anticipate your gear shifts.

Your friends shifted like this: They saw the hill and shifted into the low gear in the rear sprocket. The chain seated itself in the sprocket as they reached the gentle incline and speed was not lost. Anticipating the steep section, they shifted the front derailleur, losing a little speed, but prepared for the ascent. Now they happily cranked up the hill actually gaining a little speed as they crested the rise. Once on top, they waited for you, as all good friends will do. However, they still poked fun at your shifting!

Anticipate gear shifts in changing terrain or obstacles. Know your gearing and shift accordingly. There is nothing worse than hitting a patch of sand in high gear and trying to muscle through it.

Get used to turning, braking, slow-speed maneuvering and shifting before you hit the trail. As your skills develop, go out for short trips on easy trails or roads. Keep your speed down. Once you feel confident, then you can get gonzo and hammer!

4. THE LONG RIDE

Once you are familiar with your mountain bike, it's time to take it in the dirt. Before you go out on your first *long* ride, there are preparations that must be made. You want to be ready for anything. If your chain breaks ten miles from the nearest road; if a sudden storm hits; or if you simply just get tired, you want certain survival skills that will get you home safely.

What To Take With You And How To Carry It

Obviously, you will want to carry with you extra clothes, some food and water, a small repair kit and whatever else, camera, binoculars, etc. There are many options for different types of carriers, the most compact and portable being a small day pack. In choosing a day pack for riding, you want one with a narrow profile and a waist strap. The pack should conform to your body and not swing around as you ride. The smaller the better.

Some feel that a pack gets in the way of your movements on the bike and would rather load up the bike than themselves. There are a myriad of different bike bags, panniers, water bottle baskets and carriers. Side panniers, like the ones used in road touring, tend to get in the way on single tracks and may get wet when crossing water. A rear carrier is more practical, and the extra weight back there will add some traction. A saddlebag is nice for carrying your tool kit, but don't buy a real large one that gets in the way of a bag on the rear carrier.

A handlebar bag is a nice place to carry munchies, a map, and other necessities you may need while riding. Finally, there are frame bags that ride between the down tube and the top tube. But, don't load your bike up too much; it'll be a bear on the uphills. I usually compromise, using one or two bike bags and a small day pack or a butt bag.

Inside these bags I usually place a rain jacket or wind breaker, some gloves, (besides riding gloves), a hat, sunglasses, sun cream, and a small first aid kit. I bring a lunch or dinner, depending on how long I'm riding, some energy bars and some munchies. Always bring a lot of water, because you can get dehydrated fast and the majority of natural water holes are unsafe to drink. A light is a good idea; perhaps a clip-on battery operated light or a headlamp. Be sure it's bright enough to light your path and can be seen by other vehicles if you plan to be on the road at night.

The Tool Kit

In my tool kit, you'll find lightweight instruments, not hefty tools. I bring a crescent wrench, a pair of pliers, a screw driver for adjusting the shifters and derailleur, a tire iron, and a set of allen wrenches. Always bring an extra tube, a patch kit and a pump. A chain tool can be a godsend, for a bike without a chain is like a hiker without legs — another tool you'll be using if you are not prepared.

Shoes And Clothes

There are many types of cycling shoes, toe clips and shoe pedal combinations. Toe-clips are helpful in the city, but on the trail toe-clips get in the way. Either way, you want to wear a stout shoe. I prefer a shoe similar to the lightweight hiking boot-tennis shoes that are sold today. Some companies actually make mountain biking shoes. The shoe should have stout side walls, a narrow last, a high top and a stiff lugged sole for traction on the pedals. I like to get off my bike and hike around, so I prefer a shoe that serves both purposes.

Wear comfortable clothing or better yet, cycling clothing. These clothes are designed for mountain biking. They are padded for the crashes and have chamois cloth where your body comes in contact with the bike. They are breathable, letting sweat out, and keeping heat in. They are functional clothes designed for mountain biking.

If you are going to forgo this type of outerwear, try wearing loose clothing that you can layer on or off, depending on the temperature. Long sleeve shirts and long pants are recommendable to counter against abrasion in a fall. Better yet, use actual safety equipment.

Safety Equipment

A helmet should always be worn while riding. One day I went over the handlebars and landed on my head in soft sand. I got up giggling until I saw the basketball size granite boulder half- hidden where my helmetless head hit the dirt. Buy a full coverage helmet, with a padded inside. Don't buy one of these hairnet helmets with the three cushioned ribs. In the outback, you are dealing with a multi-dimensional surface, not a flat paved road. One sharp, narrow stone can end it for you using a hairnet helmet.

You may want to take off your helmet on a long uphill climb because it's just too hot. But the minute the road flattens out and you've got a little speed going, put it back on. And buckle it. An unbuckled helmet will fall right off in a fall. If your helmet does come in handy someday, it will probably crack. Throw it away and buy a new one. It has served you well.

Sometimes on fast descents, I'll wear knee pads or elbow pads. It adds a sense of security when there is a high risk of falling. Even a chest-guard isn't a bad idea, although it may sound like a little much. I knew a fella whose handlebars penetrated his belly. The result was a ruptured spleen. A mountain bike can kill you. It is a calculated risk. Minimize injury by staying in control and keeping your speed down.

Lock It Up

Finally, if you are riding your bike in the urban jungle, have a lock. The U-locks work best when passed through the rear wheel, the frame, and an immovable object. Chains and cable locks can be sliced easily with a pair of bolt cutters. Always lock your bike. Mountain bikes are the most often stolen bicycle.

Now, let's go on a ride.

Choose a ride that's not going to kill you. Maps, especially road maps, can be awfully deceiving. Know how to use a topographic map and plan your ride from it. A topographic map will not only show you elevation, it will show you habitations, four-wheel drive roads (where you can ride). wilderness areas (where you can't ride), and private land (where you might get shot at). You can see where there are seasonal streams and streams too big to ford. It shows you where there are forests of shade, and open views. Topographic maps are essential.

For your first long ride, go up and down the same way. Get an idea of what the terrain will be like on the descent, so there are no surprises. Also, if you grow tired on the uphill, you can simply turn around and go back the way you came. Pick a dirt road as opposed to a trail, so there is less negotiating of obstacles. And pick a classic, perhaps a ride up a canyon, or through a forest. Have a destination in mind; a lake, a spectacular view or maybe just a friend's house. Most of all have a good time!

After you've accumulated some miles under your belt, challenge yourself. Try a loop trip, riding up to a viewpoint, then down to your starting point. Hook up a network of trails, logging roads or streets to take you a different way to a familiar place. Once you have acquired the skills, there is no end to the fun you can have.

5. ADVANCED SKILLS

You are ready for a long ride. On the way, you'll find many challenges. Hills, descents, and obstacles. In this chapter, I will show you how to master these with grace and finesse. We are now out in the big bad world, not tooling around the neighborhood. These skills will allow you to ride safely and efficiently, so that you won't hurt yourself, over-exert yourself, and swear never to ride a mountain bike again. We want to build your mountain biking confidence and ability. The idea here is to have fun, and become accomplished at the skills needed to attain the exalted state of fun.

Uphill

Hill climbing may not be the most appealing part of mountain biking. Uphill is a nasty word to some people. The idea of pedaling a thirty pound machine up a steep incline does not sound enticing. Many people recall childhood memories of trying to pedal a single speed bike up a hill. Not very fun.

Yet, it is not as bad as it sounds. The mountain bike is designed for ascension; with gearing, weight shifts, and use of certain techniques, hill climbing is easier than you may think.

The gearing arrangement of mountain bikes makes hills easy. On the flats, the lowest gears seem ridiculous. You spin and spin and spin, but don't seem to go very far. Apply that gearing to a hill and amazing things happen. You seemingly can ascend anything, for hours on end, with very little difficulty. Problems arise as the hill steepens or the terrain changes. But with a little skill and a good attitude, "uphill" translates to fun.

Attitude

First of all, don't look at hill climbing negatively. Approach each hill as your own personal challenge. You're going to get to the top, no matter what. You may have to stop and rest once in a while, even walk the bike, but next time you'll climb this same hill continuously. The top is your reward. Be motivated when you climb hills.

Keep It Up

You can get motivated by setting up for the hill properly. As you approach the hill, develop a strong spin. Now, as the terrain grows steeper and you must down shift, keep your rpm's up. Shift early enough so that you aren't exerting a lot of force to maintain that spin. You should be exerting the same amount of force after the gear change as you did before the gear change. You probably will slow down, but that's O.K. The idea is to maintain your rate of spin and exert the same amount of force, no matter which gear you shift into. You want to get up the hill as efficiently as possible.

Keep Going, Even If It's Steep

As the hill gets really steep, you may find yourself in your lowest gear, quickly losing your cadence. You try standing in the saddle but find that the tire skids out in the dirt. Sit down. Your weight over the rear wheel adds traction. It also helps to raise your seat for climbs; it adds more power to the pedals. Sitting on the seat, your knees should be slightly bent.

Sometimes, if the riding surface is firm, you can stand in the

Figure 11
Sitting back in the saddle gives more traction.

saddle and lean slightly back to add traction. You may try pulling the bike from side to side to increase the force on each stroke of the pedal. If you have toe-clips, pull up on them to add force. Keep it up.

The Line

It is important to pick a good line when climbing. Try and keep the bike as straight as possible. Turning the front wheel from side to side to keep your balance reduces your momentum. Try pulling mini-wheelies to reduce friction and add even more traction. Look ahead and try to gauge the terrain before you get there. Avoid sandy spots and ruts. If you must climb through them, keep the bike straight.

Practice

As you try steeper or sandier hills, you might get discouraged. Keep on trying to ride them as practice, even though you may have to rest often. A hill that you've ascended many times is always easier than the first time. Apply the techniques you have learned to the most severe situations.

Starting Up, Again

When you start out on a hill, you must immediately develop a strong spin to keep the bike going. Get on the bike, place one foot on the pedal and press down hard. Use the other foot to keep you in balance, then quickly push down on the other pedal. If you stop between strokes, you will instantly lose momentum and lose your balance.

Too Steep

All right, so the hill is just too steep to climb. Go ahead and walk the bike. Sometimes a little walking is what you need to rest up enough so you can try riding again. But let's face it, some hills are just too steep to ride. Keep walking.

Walking the bike also takes a little skill. Don't push the bike using both handlebars. This is inefficient, for all your force is being applied to the front wheel while the rear wheel drags. Hold onto

Figure 12
When it is too steep to ride, walk the bike.

the closest handlebar and the back of the seat. I like to apply most of the force to the rear, and just keep the bike straight with the front. This way, the front wheel tends to bounce over stones and obstacles while the rear wheel gets lifted over.

If you must carry the bike, hoist it onto your shoulder with one arm and keep the handlebars out of your face with the other arm. Thirty pounds of mountain bike can be a lot to carry over distance, so you may want a shoulder pad. You can purchase a pad that doubles as a carrier. It hangs between the top tube and the seat tube. But, we prefer to ride the bike not carry it. So if there is a lot of carrying involved, you may want to pick another route.

I know of a ride where one mile of walking up hill brings you nine miles of the best downhill you could imagine. The ascent winds up a steep talus field of boulders and sand. You walk and sometimes carry your bike up. At the top, you are greeted by alpine meadows, groves of pines and firm, level trails. Soon the trail drops back into the canyon, through fields of aspen, granite boulders and incredible winding roads. It's time to learn some descending skills.

Descending

Descending is the most thrilling part of mountain bike riding. Gravity provides the thrill, you provide the skill. The objective: don't fall down. It is a balancing act. You don't have to go fast. Just stay in control. Speed comes with skill. If you want to go fast, know what you are doing. The expert downhiller is the one who does not get hurt.

In the Kamikaze! downhill race, expert riders reach speeds of 60 mph. Citizen riders average about 30 mph. The citizen rider will be decked out in padding, guards, and protectors. The expert wears nothing except a helmet. Why? Because the experts do not fall.

If there is one thing to remember about descents, it is to stay in control. You can really push it and hurt yourself badly. Know your ability, your bike, and the descent. Be cautious. You can still go fast, but be reasonable.

First, make sure your bike is in proper working order. Be sure your brakes are tight. Loose brakes may not provide enough braking force, and can be forced beneath the rim, rendering the brakes

Figure 13
Downhill riding stance.

useless. Tighten your wheels. Check your derailleurs. The tires should be true. One bump and a wobbly wheel can collapse. This bike is going to be put through some abuse.

Before you start the descent, lower the seat for more traction. Your riding stance should be upright and relaxed. Shift slightly to the rear of the seat to keep traction and place your pedals horizontally. As you hit bumps and ruts, absorb the shock by rising slightly off the seat.

The majority of the shock will be absorbed at the handlebars, so you want to be sure to keep your hands loose, yet firm enough so that the bars don't get jerked out of your hands. Form your hands into a ring with your thumb and index fingers touching. The other fingers will ride over the brakes. Let the handlebar jerk around in the ring created by your hands, while steering with the thumb and index fingers. Tighten up on all the fingers as you brake. Try to brake in rhythmic pumps, not quick spurts. A quick pull on the brakes will skid your tires or worse, send you over the handlebars. Stay relaxed and you won't make mistakes.

Terrain Changes On Descents

Keep looking about twenty yards ahead. Anticipate your next move. Try and judge the approaching terrain and ride accordingly. Washboards are easy. Keep your weight back and just ride over them. Pinch the front of the seat with your thighs to add stability. Ruts get trickier. Try and stay out of places where water has carved little canyons into the surface. If you find yourself in a rut, don't try and steer out of it immediately. Your front wheel can get stuck and flip you over. Reduce your speed by braking slowly. Look for a place where the sides of the rut are not steep and exit there. If you can, avoid getting into a rut in the first place.

Gravel And Rocky Roads

Gravelly roads can be very scary. You have less traction on gravel yet can travel just as fast as on dirt. Keep your speed down on curves, perhaps going into a controlled skid in the tighter turns. Don't move around a lot while riding gravel. Stand on the pedals and pinch the seat with your thighs. Try and keep the bike riding upright and straight.

Rocky roads hurt. A large rock may impede progress and flip you over. It is often hard to judge how fast you can go through rocky sections. Be cautious. If you enter at a fast rate of speed, sit way back on the seat, almost over the rear tire, and ride it out. Braking suddenly can throw you down. Anticipate the terrain and slow down before you get there.

Steep Descents

Really steep descents call for caution. If it is long and steep, go slow. Keep the brakes on, releasing them slowly, to let you down easy. Keep your feet out and touching the ground to prevent the wheels from sliding out. Avoid obstacles for they might send you crashing. Once you can see where the road flattens out, begin to increase your speed again.

If it is a short and steep descent, coast through it without braking. Braking suddenly on steep terrain will cause you to fall. Enter the steep section at a safe rate of speed for you will pick up speed as you coast through it.

Sand

Sand can make a bike squirrelly and slow it down instantly. Soft spots will flip you. The best way to approach sand is to maintain a low, rear-weighted stance as in riding rocky sections. The important thing is to keep the bike straight while riding through the sand. It is advisable to reduce your speed before entering the sandy section, grasp the handlebars with all your fingers, hold on tight and ride it out. At least when you fall in sand, it's a soft landing.

Obstacles On Descents

Be aware of obstacles in the roadway and to the sides. A branch can get stuck in your spokes. Hidden holes will toss you to the ground. It may be difficult to see obstacles as you go in and out of the shade. Adjust your speed so that you can be totally aware of changes in terrain. Also, watch what is to the sides of the road. If you must make a quick evasive maneuver you don't want to hit a tree or a boulder.

Be committed as you ride through obstacles. You either have to blast over them or slow down and safely negotiate the obstacle. Keep looking ahead of you, keeping your weight back, your stance low, and prepared for anything.

Cornering On Descents

Corners can be tricky on descents. The two most often made mistakes are overshooting the corner and skidding out or flipping from improper weight distribution. As you enter the corner, look ahead and try to judge how fast you can take it, and where your line will be in order to maintain that speed. Adjust your speed before you enter the corner and lean (not steer) towards the apex of the turn. Be sure your pedals are aligned vertically, with the downward pedal towards the outside of the turn.   If you have entered the turn too fast, slowly brake as you enter the apex, not as you exit the turn. Otherwise, you'll overshoot the turn and find yourself in the bushes. If you brake and turn simultaneously, you may skid out or flip because of the lean you are placing upon the bike.

At the apex of the turn there are many different techniques you can use. You can take a tighter line, brake hard, skidding out the rear wheel at the apex. You may take an outside line, describing a larger arc, then drop into the apex with a straight line through the turn. Likewise, you may come into the apex on a straight tack, then skid or turn out on the outside of the turn. Your choice is dependent upon the terrain in the turn and your speed as you enter the turn.

If it is soft on the outside of a turn, drop into the apex to avoid it. If it's soft at the apex, a tight turn may be warranted to blast through it. If you are entering a pair of S curves, a straight line as you exit the turn will set you up for the next curve.

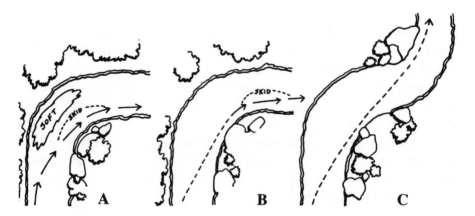

Figure 14
A)   Outside turn
B)   Inside turn
C)   S-curve — Pick out straight line.

Out Of Control

So you're bombing down a hill and suddenly find yourself out of control. The best thing to do is to try and slow down without skidding. Brake slowly and try to keep the bike riding on a straight line, even if it means riding off the road. A sudden turn may tumble you. Slow down to a complete stop and start over. Oftentimes you think you have reduced your speed enough without stopping, only to find yourself out of control again. Stop and catch your breath. Always be cautious on descents.

Just because it's a descent doesn't mean you have to go fast. But if you are going to fly down hills, know some technique. Practice descending wearing knee pads, elbow pads and a helmet. As you get better, push it a little. But always stay in control. Those of you who are sane and don't need to go fast, use these techniques to keep upright and have fun!

6. OBSTACLES

Mountain bikes are unbelievable tools that can ride over logs, through boulders and into streams. It takes a little skill, but is a wonderful talent that can be mastered with little difficulty. To become skilled at obstacles, know the limitations of your bike and what it needs to clear certain obstacles.

First, be sure and have the proper safety equipment when riding over obstacles. Riding obstacles is a delicate balancing act that can result in injury. Always wear a helmet, and maybe even knee pads and elbow pads. Put some knee pads around your shins. Sometimes your feet slip off the pedals and the pedals can strike your shins. Always be ready for a mistake with an outstretched leg or arm. In a complete roll-over, try and get away from the obstacle and the bike. Falling from atop an obstacle can be devastating.

Before you try riding obstacles, gain an understanding of how a bike clears an obstacle. Get off your bike and walk it over the obstacle. Watch where the bicycle clears an obstacle and where it does not. Understand the forces involved to get it up and over the obstacle.

The Log

The most basic obstacle is the log. A small log is easy to negotiate. Pull a small wheelie over the log and throw your weight forward to get the rear wheel over the log. As you come off the log, shift your center of gravity to the rear of the bike. Obstacles can be broken into three parts: enough speed to get up, enough momentum to get over and proper weight distribution to descend. These principals can be applied to any obstacle.

Try walking the bike over a larger log (about 12" — 24" in height). Lift gently on the handlebars and bring the front wheel over the log. It will look like the chain ring is about to hit the top of the log. But as the front wheel descends one side of the log, the rear wheel has already begun to rise above the log, clearing the chain ring. On a smaller log, the front wheel will be on the ground before the rear wheel can get up the log and the chain ring will not clear. Obviously, the larger the log the easier it will be to clear the chain ring. The problem lies in getting up on the log in the first place.

It takes a lot of force to get up on the log. Ride towards it at a good clip and pull a wheelie, landing your front wheel atop the log. Now, at this point, your bike will come to a complete stop — unless you throw your weight forward with the momentum of the bike. This pushes the bike over the log and brings your rear wheel atop the log.

You want to be sure that your pedals are set upright as you mount the log. Keep them vertical as you pull the wheelie and push them to horizontal at the exact moment you throw your weight forward. Do not pedal to vertical, as your pedal is sure to hit the log. Once your front wheel is over the log, begin pedaling again.

As you descend, you want to shift your weight back so you don't flip over the front. Sit back as far as possible behind the seat, so your rear-end is almost touching the rear tire. Your center of gravity should be over the obstacle as you ride over it. Once on the ground, center yourself back over the bike.

Momentum and balance must work together in clearing obstacles. You need enough momentum to get over the obstacle, while at the same time keeping your balance. Too little momentum will stop you; too much and it's dirt for lunch. As you practice, you'll get an idea of what it takes to get you up and over.

Another technique is to grind the teeth of your chain ring into the log and pedal over it. Although this technique is effective on flatter logs, you are sure to damage your chain ring doing this. Anyway you look at it, you are bound to hit your chain ring practicing obstacles. Look at your chain ring as a disposable item; buy cheap ones if you will be attempting obstacles. I replace my chain ring every few months.

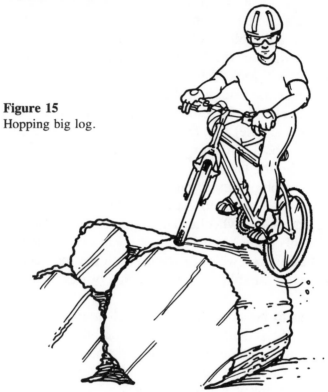

Figure 15
Hopping big log.

Hopping Over A Log

As the log gets bigger, it is more difficult to get enough momentum to get atop it. The hopping technique may be used. Although very difficult to master, hopping can get a bicycle up and over a log that is bigger than the bike itself. Hopping differs from the techniques just described because the cyclist does not ride up and over the obstacle in one continuous motion. In hopping, momentum is broken down into moves, each move concentrating on getting a certain part of the bike up and over the log one at a time.

Crucial to this technique is the ability to balance the bike between moves. To do this, the bike must be completely stationary. This technique is as difficult to master as hopping, but is essential in getting over large obstacles. It is a technique that must be practiced and built upon, first by riding to a complete stop and attempting to balance. It is much easier to balance if the bike is moving slightly. Pedal a little, then stop, shifting your weight backwards. Once mastered, you will be able to integrate this with hopping to clear large obstacles.

To clear a large log, you must pull a wheelie and land the front wheel atop the log, pulling on the brakes to stop the bike falling backwards off the log. Now push your momentum forward, and hop the rear wheel on top of the log, again braking and remaining stationary atop the log. Now, ride off the log with your weight as far back as possible. Much easier said than done.

The Log Bridge

A log bridge is scary, yet not as difficult as it looks. Approach the log at a good clip, and get both wheels onto it steering straight. Continue to pedal the length of the log, keeping the wheel straight. Balance comes from forward enertia, not your steering ability. So be sure and be in a gear that is applying power to the bike and not just coasting across. If you feel as if you are going to fall, try and get away from the bike.

These techniques have advanced into a sub-sport of mountain biking called Trials. Trials involves mastering obstacles without the aid of your feet for balance. Blending the techniques of free-style trick riding and mountain biking, Trials is far removed from what we might encounter in our daily mountain bike excursion. Trials riders are able to hop up an obstacle, and jump off from ten feet up, completing a full 360 degree rotation before landing. Since trials is really a completely different sport from mountain biking, this book will not attempt to describe the more advanced techniques of trials riding, even though they can be done on a mountain bike.

Hopping and standing, however, are techniques you can use in your everyday rides. Perfecting these techniques will make obstacles easier. Especially when attempting boulders and rock obstacles.

Figure 16
Log crossing sequence.
A) Pop a wheelie to place the front wheel on the log.
B) Throw your weight forward to bring the back wheel on the log.
C) Put your weight back and ride off.

Boulders, Rocks And Hard Knocks

Boulders are approached just like logs, except for one difference: they are not as uniform, hence they can be more difficult. In going over large boulders, I scout out all sides of the rock, looking for the lowest angled side. I ascend on this side and descend a steeper side. Avoid riding over the summit of the boulder and descending. You are bound to hit the chain ring on the summit. Instead, look for a place where the boulder flattens out before steepening for the descent.

Often the ascent and descent of the boulder will not be in a straight line so a small turn may have to be made. Make this turn

36

by steering, not leaning. Try and keep your balance as upright as possible to avoid falling off the boulder.

On large boulders that you must go up and over, it is best to be in a low gearing, but not so low that your pedal strokes won't provide enough power to get you up and over the boulder. And remember to align your pedals where clearance might be a problem. Keeping them horizontal as you go over the top is best.

On smaller boulders, back pedaling helps to give you clearance. A full rotation of the pedals may cause the pedal to strike the rock. Place your pedals horizontal where you need clearance, then pedal a half stoke to give you power. Back pedal one-half revolution to avoid striking the pedal, then pedal forward over rock. This way you avoid striking the pedal on the rock, while at the same time giving power to the bike.

Pedals are another disposable item. Like it or not, they get pretty bashed up. There are some pedals that are quite sturdy and take a lot of abuse. However, in a severe impact, some pedals may bend within the crank and pull out, stripping the crank or breaking off in the crank themselves. I use plastic pedals that simply break upon impact. When there is not enough pedal to stand on, I throw them away. You may not be so harsh on your pedals and prefer a sturdy metal pedal. Equipment choice is a matter of personal preference. Just be ready to lose a few pedals.

You might have to ride through a series of large rocks. It is

Figure 17
Riding over boulders.

a matter of picking the best line to get through the obstacle. It is best to try and weave the front tire through rocks and let the rear tire ride up and over them. This requires standing up on the pedals and throwing your weight forward as the rear tire hits the rock. Sometimes you can aim it just right so that the front wheel passes to one side of the rock, the chain ring passes over the rock and the rear wheel passes to the opposite side of the rock.

Water

Water crossings are fun. They'll cool you off on that long hot ride, without getting your feet wet. The bike actually carves a path through the water, spraying your torso and keeping your feet dry. However, one mistake in a water crossing and you may get more than just your feet wet.

It is best to examine the water crossing carefully before attempting it. Hidden boulders or sudden deep spots will sink you. Most water crossings appear at pools in the streams and have similar characteristics. The water is dammed by boulders and rocks on the downstream side of the pool. Sand collects against these rocks with other rocks lying against the upstream side of the pool. You want to avoid hitting any large rocks as you go through the pool, and likewise, you do not want to get bogged down in the sand. The best place to cross is that point between sand and rocks, where the bottom of the stream is consistent and smooth.

Approach the stream at a good rate of speed, coasting into it. The water will slow you down considerably. As your speed drops, start pedaling. Be sure that you are in a low gear, but not so low that you can't get any power. Keep your weight over the rear tire for maximum traction. As you begin to rise out of the stream, drop to a lower gear and stand up as you gain traction on the dry ground.

A very fast rate of speed will cause the bike to hydro-plane on the water, actually skim across the surface. This is very dangerous, for you really do not have any control over the bike until you've reached dry ground on the other side. Try riding through streams before attempting to hydro-plane the bike.

Most mountain bikes are equipped with sealed-bearing hubs and bottom brackets, that keep moisture out of these areas. If your bike does not have a sealed system, riding through water can hurt the bike. The grease inside will run out of the hubs and your bearings will be grinding against the unlubricated axle. In non- sealed bearing systems, never immerse the bottom bracket or hubs totally in the water.

Figure 18
Water crossings are fun.

Snow And Ice

Where I live, twenty foot snowstorms are not uncommon. With that much snow, the plows have a tough time keeping the roads clear. Autos are marooned, yet mountain bikes flourish. Riding in thick snow is easy. The snow provides unbelievable traction. When things get icy, it gets dangerous. If you hit a patch of ice and you feel the bike starting to go, place both feet firmly on the ice and let the bike fall from beneath you. Balance on your feet and skate out of it. This is strictly a survival technique that is difficult to perform. Try to avoid riding on ice to begin with.

Although rocks, logs and water are the most common obstacles when trail riding, there are others. Curbs, drains, cars, dogs, pot holes are more urban types of obstacles. These will be dealt with in another chapter. But the approach is similar. You can use the same technique for descending a boulder as you do for descending stairs. Just be safe when attempting obstacles. Scout the obstacle, wear safety gear, and don't get in over your head. You might land on your head. Be safe and have fun.

7. ALL-TERRAIN

The term mountain bike is incorrect. These bikes are not exclusive to the mountains. They are perfect for city riding, across the farm, or along the beach. They are really All-Terrain Bikes, also known as ATB's. Mountain bikes can be ridden over many types of terrain and the handling characteristics change for each type of terrain encountered. In this chapter we will discuss the differences between riding a trail and a road, over slick rock or the beach, and the places you should not ride — like over the neighbor's lawn, for instance.

Mountain Bike Etiquette

Unfortunately, many people have connotations of mountain bikes as destructive machines bombing across country, scaring wildlife and livestock, wreaking havoc upon all who come in its path. Most mountain bikers are quite the opposite; nature loving people, who use the bike as a tool to get them to beautiful places. Undoubtedly, you will encounter other people in the back country, who may harbor ill-will against you. Or perhaps they have never seen a mountain bike, and this is your chance to educate them.

A code of proper behavior on a mountain bike has been created for you to follow. Abide by these guidelines, for you are an ambassador of mountain biking. Demonstrate that mountain bikes and mountain bikers are not the vermin of the back country.

The mountain biker's code, as defined by the **National Off-Road Bicyclist Association (NORBA)**, is as follows:

1) I will yield the right of way to other non-motorized recreationalists.

2)   I will use caution when over taking another and will make my presence known well in advance.

3)   I will maintain control of my speed at all times.

4)   I will stay on designated trails.

5)   I will not disturb wildlife and livestock.

6)   I will not litter.

7)   I will respect public and private property.

8)   I will always be self-sufficient.

9)   I will not travel solo when bikepacking in remote areas.

10)   I will observe the practice of minimum impact bicycling.

11)   I will always wear a helmet when I ride.

Single Track

Treat the land and those who use it with respect. This means minimum impact. Pick up your garbage, don't pollute streams and lakes with soap or wastes, never ride across meadows or fields. Where animals are grazing, always close gates behind you and stay away from the livestock. Mountain bikes have been restricted access to many places. Let's show the public that we care.

Trails have become known as single tracks in mountain bike jargon. Dirt roads, with their dual grooves are double tracks, although they are not regularly called this. The single track provides some of the most exciting riding for a couple of reasons. First, you are not going to encounter any automobiles on the single track, and depending on where you ride, maybe no motorcycles either. The single track tends to be more technical because of its narrowness and limited line of sight. Hence, you need to keep your speed down on single tracks, because a surprise obstacle or hiker might mean a nasty collision.

Single tracks may be a trail in your local park, or a hiking trail in the mountains. Before you begin, find out if it is legal to ride a mountain bike on the trail. Many parks, national forests and recreation areas have banned mountain bikes on their trails. There are many reasons; the most often cited is conflicts with other trail users like hikers or horses and trail erosion. Conflicts can be mitigated by careful riding, keeping your speed down and being aware of other trail users. In fact, on trails where there are other users, I find it best to dismount and let them pass as a courtesy. Put your best foot forward so that other trail users don't get a bad impression of mountain bikers.

Do mountain bikes cause erosion? Not any more than any other trail users. Horses cause the most erosion. The constant pounding of horseshoes makes trails very sandy, as does the passing of many hiking boots. Mountain bikes have the opposite effect; they compact the trail. However, skidding mountain bikes loosen the soil. But on the single track, we should keep our speed down, so skidding the bike should not occur. The question needs some unbiased research.

Presently, many trails are closed to mountain bikes that should not be. Write your congressman or park manager. To ban mountain bikes from all trails is a blatant form of discrimination.

Once you've determined that it's legal to ride on the trail, determine who else might be using it. Horses and bikes are not compatible. Horses are easily spooked by mountain bikes, so keep your speed down. Increase your speed only when you have good view. As you approach corners, slow down. Often corners will be tight, so you will want to keep it slow anyway.

You'll often find the center of the trail very sandy. Ride up on the edge of the trail where it is more compact, taking care not to ride **off** the trail. Where there is a water bar in the trail, (a stone or log placed across the trail to divert run- off) ride over the water bar, not off the trail around it. Never ride off the trail. This **does** create erosion.

There may be branches or plants leaning into the trail. Be careful. A branch can easily put your eye out. Duck down as you approach these obstacles. A branch at handlebar height really hurts when it swipes the hand. Although gloves help, practice riding with one hand and lifting the other hand out of the way. But watch it. You can easily fall riding one-handed.

Switchbacks

Single tracks will often have switchbacks, places where the trail switches directions as it traverses a slope. The switchback is difficult to ride around. Going upward, you must give the bike a lot of power, and abruptly stop pedaling as you start to make your turn. Turn the front wheel 45 degrees to the bike and start pedaling again. The key here is to slow down enough to make that tight

Figure 19
Switchback turn.

turn. If you're going too fast, the front wheel will dig in and you'll stop. If you are going too slow, you'll fall over.

Going down the switchback is trickier. The same principle applies, however if you lean too far forward you will flip over the handlebars. You need to keep your weight back as you slow down for the turn, then lean into the turn once you've turned the handlebars. Keep the brakes on, letting them out in spurts as you go around the switchback.

The single track is a wonderful part of mountain biking. Just be sure you are allowed on the trail and that you don't ruin any other trail user's day. Keep your speed down, especially when visibility is limited.

Dirt Roads

Dirt roads can be just as enjoyable as the single track. Many forests have logging roads that wind around forever. But don't become a member of the dead-end gang. Many logging roads will lead to dead-ends that may be agonizing to retrace. Have a map with you, especially on logging roads.

The age old question concerning dirt roads is which track do

I ride in? You want to avoid riding in loose sandy soil and stick to the track that has firm and compacted dirt. Sand and debris collect where the flow of water is impeded. Hence the lower of the two tracks will usually have silt and debris in it. The higher track will be more compact and easier to ride in. Also, the steeper the track, the more compact it is likely to be, with sand piling up at the bottom of hills. Beware of this sudden sandbox.

To pick the perfect line on a double track, you must be looking ahead, scanning the terrain. If a soft spot, or a pile of rocks lay within your track, you must be ready to switch tracks. The center of the road between tracks is often soft and covered in brush. At

Figure 20
Dirt roadtrack switch.
A)   NO
B)   YES

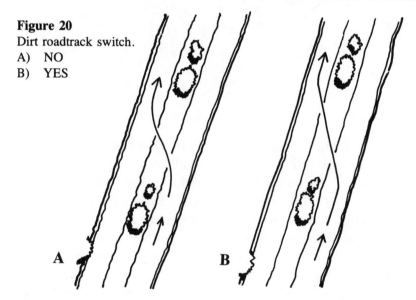

high speeds, the center will catch your front wheel and throw you to the ground. Try and pick a place to cross the center that seems less brushy and most compact. Turn diagonally and ride a straight line through it. Do not turn across the center. Start your turn in one track, ride diagonally across the center, and make your next turn after you enter the new track.

Slick Rock

Slick rock is a unique geological phenomenon that occurs in sandstone. Erosion has created smooth hills and bowls interspersed by an occasional patch of sand. The landscape is eerie and strange, yet great to ride on.

The Slick Rock Trail in Moab, Utah is a mountain biker's classic. Originally created for motorcycles, the trail has become a mountain biking mecca. Painted on the surface of the rock is a dashed white line that is followed for the length of the trail. It winds up, down and around a sandstone plateau above the translucent Colorado River. Along the way, you pass by Indian petroglyphs, delicate wind sculpted arches and outstanding views of canyon country.

Riding on slick rock can be compared to riding on pavement, except it is slippery. Every surface is slick and hard, demanding careful riding technique. Locking your brakes up on a downhill can result in a nasty case of slick rock rash. It is best to approach downhills slowly, keeping your speed down. If you want to go all out, don't lock the brakes. Just be sure you have enough room to slow down on the flats.

Riding uphill also can be difficult. Since you are riding on a hard surface, the trail takes you up some very steep pitches. Your instinct is to stand out of the saddle and lean forward, but this will cause your rear wheel to spin out on the slick surface. Approach the steep hill with speed, sitting down as you ride up it, then standing up as the angle of the hill lessens.

Moab is not the only place you'll find slick rock. Similar formations can be found all over the country on granite, limestone, etc. These techniques will help you wherever the surface is extremely hard and smooth.

Sand, Pumice And Other Nasties

There is only one good thing that can be said about riding in sand. When you fall, it's a soft landing. Otherwise, sand can be very difficult to ride in. Everyone rides through patches of sand once in a while, but what do you do when the entire trail is one big sand trough? Pick another trail ...

Seriously, some of us are not blessed with trails that are always firm. You may live near a beach, in a desert or close to a volcanic area that has a lot of pumice sand. Riding on these surfaces takes patience and determination. Sand creates a lot of resistance against the bike. The idea is to minimize that resistance.

Always try and keep a straight line when riding through the sand. The more you move around the more resistance you create against the sand, decreasing efficiency. Sit as far back on the bike as you can, keeping your weight over the rear wheel.

When it really gets deep, you may try pulling little wheelies. This decreases resistance by pulling the front wheel momentarily out of the sand. Keep pumping. No one said that riding the soft stuff was easy.

Descents can be tricky. Again, maintain a straight line. Don't make sudden movements, especially in curves. Make your turns fluid and wide. Be prepared for variations in the sand. Deep sand will slow you down instantly, possibly throwing you off the bike. By keeping your weight to the rear of the bike and riding a straight line, you can plow through deep sand without incident.

On climbs, the same rules apply. Ride a straight line and keep your weight to the rear by sitting down. Standing out of the saddle is ineffective. Keep it up. Determination and patience are the best techniques you can use in sand.

The Urban Jungle

The majority of mountain bikes will be used in the canyons of the city, on rivers of pavement and through forests of automobiles and pedestrians. The mountain bike is well suited for the city; potholes, curbs and sewer grates can be handled with ease. With all the controls at your finger tips, increased stability, and a high point of view, the mountain bike is perfect for city riding.

The first rule of city riding is to be seen. Wear bright clothing, or have an antenna flag, so cars can see you. At night have reflective clothing as well as rear and front lights. Remember that traffic is usually travelling at twice or three times the speed you are. Signal your intentions well before you make the move with hand signals. Avoid riding in the car's blind spot: the right rear corner of an automobile. Always be ready to make an evasive maneuver. Often-times cars don't know that you are there until it is too late.

Awareness is important in city riding. Look to all sides or have a rear view mirror. At intersections, be aware of the right turner. He'll cut you off, crushing your front wheel or worse. In slow traffic it is best to stay ahead of a car where you can be seen, or well behind a car where you have time to get out of the way.

In most states, the bike has the same rights and responsibilities as autos. That means obeying all traffic rules. Remember that pedestrians always have the right of way. However, if you are riding in a crosswalk you do not have the same rights as pedestrians unless you are walking the bike. This is the only time a cyclist can be considered a pedestrian.

Always stay to the far right of the roadway. It is arguable that on winding roads it is safer to ride against traffic, but the law is the law. Stay right. If you are holding up a line of cars, pull off the road. After all, you are on a mountain bike. Treat the shoulder as another type of terrain!

Obstacles like curbs, stairs and puddles can be treated the same as logs, boulders and water crossings. But one of the greatest obstacles in city riding is the unleashed dog. The best way to handle a violent canine is ignorance and speed. Do not heed his barks and keep pedaling. Once you've passed his territory he'll give up. Just keep your eyes ahead of you, and not on the jowls nipping at your heels.

Occasionally, these animals must be taught a lesson. Stopping the bike at a safe distance and holding your ground often scares a dog into complacency. A swift kick in the face or a swipe with your pump should only be used in the most extreme instances of self defense. Carrying a couple of dog biscuits with you is a friendlier tact. If you are bitten, report the incident to local animal control authorities and have the bite looked at by a doctor.

Always lock your bike in the city. Leave it alone for a second and it's gone. Be careful in rough neighborhoods. I once had a gang of cyclists come up to me and claim that I was riding "their" bike. I held my ground and like the excited canine, they left me alone. Be defensive, in attitude and in your cycling.

Riding a bike around a city is the best way to get to know it. Stick to bike paths, if possible. Many Chambers of Commerce have bike maps for cities that show the best routes. Go to the museum, the park or to work on your bike and have fun!

8. COMPETITION

Mountain bike racing consists of a variety of events; down-hills, hill-climbs, observed trials, circuit races, dual challenge (like a slalom ski race) and cross-country races. In most races, anyone can participate. You are categorized by your racing experience, age and type of bike. The different classes are Beginner (never have raced); Intermediate (have raced 5 races); Experts (have placed in three races or have six top finishes in six races); Super (top level amateurs; Single Speed Bike; Stock Bike (Trials); Modified Bike (Trials); Junior (under 18); Veteran (35-45); Masters (45 and up). You can be classified in three categories in each event, e.g. Single Speed, Expert, Masters.

Mountain bike racers have become specialists in certain events. Some are better hillclimbers, others love the downhill. Observed trials riding has really become a separate sport from mountain bike racing and many racers prefer not to enter this event. This has led to two methods of scoring events. The first method scores each event individually. In other words, your place on the downhill will have no effect on your place in the cross-country.

The second method of scoring is the stage race. The stage race is where you combine your score in each race to come up with an overall winner for the event. Regardless of how the winner is determined, most mountain bike racers will agree that winning isn't everything. Mountain bike competition is a friendly gathering where everyone helps each other. For example, the World Mountain Bike championships held in Mammoth Lakes, CA.

The Hillclimb

I once rode this climb for a pleasure ride. It was not pleasurable. The road surface is thick pumice and volcanic rock making traction difficult. Oftentimes, I got off my bike and walked. I would get back on the bike, pedal for a few hundred yards and feel the thin air of altitude burn in my lungs. I made it though, riding my bike up and over the rock cairn that marked the 11,053 foot summit. So I didn't ride it the entire way, but I did finish it. The view from the top was well worth it.

But for the race, things are different. The road has been graded and everyone is conditioned to the altitude after a season of racing. The start gun goes off and the racers charge out at 25 mph. They stay in a close pack, take advantage of each other's draft, exchanging the lead to give everyone an equal advantage.

The strategy for a hillclimb is to pace yourself so that you don't get too tired for the top. This is one bike race where drafting comes into play. Tucking yourself in behind other riders decreases wind resistance, providing more power. If you are like me, you won't be able to keep up with the pack and find yourself strung out along the course. Don't push yourself. Get into a rhythm, enjoy the views, and just finish the race.

The Cross-Country Race

The cross-country race at Mammoth is really a circuit race, although it travels across the countryside. You rise 500 feet in two miles to Reds Lake, spin around the lake, and gain the single track for two miles along the rim of the San Joaquin River Valley. Then the single track makes a sharp descent, winding around thick jeffery pines to the finish. At the finish you are greeted by a large bump that will send you flying. The pros and experts run five revolutions while the amateur riders go around thrice.

At the start, everyone is together in a pack. But by Reds Lake the Pros and Experts have left the amateur riders far behind. No one expects the sharp turn at Reds Lake. Many of the amateur riders are sent over their handlebars into the water. On the single-track, the action is fast and furious. Riders bomb through the woods at 40 mph, then stop and push their bikes up the next hill. The descent on the backside is equally as hairaising. The twisting course demands a tight line and a keen eye, lest you become emblazoned on the bark of a pine tree.

Ned Overend pulls away from the pack at Reds Lake followed by John Tomac. At the end of the first lap, the two are far from the pack and soon laps amateur riders. They politely ask the cyclists to move out of the way so they can move through, and the cyclists comply.

Suddenly, Ned hears the hissing of air and pulls out with a flat. He is passed by Tomac and the pack. Unlike road racing, there is not a free lap for technical difficulty. Ned has to fix the tire as quickly as possible and get back in the race, fighting his way up to the front. This rule simulates a verity of mountain bike riding. Self-sufficiency. If you are out there and something goes wrong, you'd better be prepared.

Unfortunately, some beginner riders did not understand the camaraderie of mountain bike racing as Tomac tried to make his way to the front. On the single track, where passing is almost impossible, these riders would not let Tomac pass! Although Tomac finished the race, he did not place due to the insensitivity of some riders. Although a leading rider "owns the track," you always let a stronger rider pass; it is an unwritten rule.

Finally, on the last lap, Overend re-gained the lead and finished in first. He won because he played his cards right. He was prepared with tool kit and tire repair. He passed riders where the road was wide, and held his ground in the single track. His excellent handling skills and boundless energy enabled him to fight his way back to the front. In cross-country races, it is best to hang back and save it up for the end — hoping you don't run into technical trouble. If you do, you must be prepared.

The Dual Challenge

A ski area has a lot of earth moving equipment to build ski runs, so why not build a race course for mountain bikes? This course has been designed specifically for this event and will be removed once the race is over. The dual challenge starts with two starting gates on a blue and a red course. The riders race against each other through a series of elimination rounds, switching courses each time. The winner is the rider who has won the most races.

The dual challenge brings every mountain bike skill into one fast race. Shifting, descents, climbing, obstacles and curves present themselves at the same time. The major difficulty is shifting. A racer must jump between high and low gears in a matter of seconds, while handling his bike around turns and over bumps. Often the racer finds himself trying to crank up the hill in a high gear because he didn't shift in time. Bike handling is a given. You are supposed to be able to negotiate the obstacles. It doesn't always work out that way. Crashes are bound to happen making this an exciting race to watch.

The Observed Trials

Negotiating obstacles is an obvious component of mountain biking. Observed Trials arose out of this necessity. Cyclists test their handling skills through a series of obstacles that mimic the obstacles they might encounter in the woods.

However, as skill levels increased, the obstacles became more outrageous. A skilled trials rider of today would make quick work of a Volkswagon — riding up its bumper to the hood, hopping onto the roof, then descending the engine cover.

Each movement of the trials rider is observed by a judge, hence the name "Observed Trials." The rider negotiates a series of obstacles called a section. The goal is to "clean" the section, complete it without putting a foot down, called a "dab." Each dab represents a point. Five points are given for putting your foot down and impeding forward motion. The rider with the lowest number of points is the winner.

Obviously, a bicycle that is designed for trials riding will fare a lot better than the average mountain bike. Trials bikes resemble BMX or freestyle bikes. They are lightweight, with a small chain ring for clearance. Some don't even have a seat, for the trial rider rarely sits down. They have short stubby handle bars and fat tires that are almost fully deflated. These features allow the trials rider to hop the bike easier, clear obstacles and remain stationary longer.

In most races, they have two categories of trial entrants, stock bikes and modified trials bikes. Different courses are designed for each. The stock bike course tends to go through boulders, streams, and over logs. The modified bike course is the eye catcher. It may contain huge boulders as tall as a man, bridges composed of loose bouncing boards, and leaps to the ground from fifteen feet up. These are accomplished smoothly with perhaps an extra twist thrown in for show.

Figure 22
Observed trails.

In some ways, the stock course gets back to the original concept of mountain biking. It's you and the bike out there, and you've got to get through that obstacle alive. When we encounter a log in the woods, we don't switch bikes, and start hopping over it, we make do with what we have. In Crested Butte, Colorado, the trials course is completely natural. It is held in an aspen grove outside of town. The sections thread between tight trees, balance across a log bridge, or slosh up a boulder-filled creek. A trials bike here would be a disadvantage. As a mountain bike event, trials riding should be done on a mountain bike and practiced in mountainous terrain. Riding modified bikes over crazy obstacles is a circus act whose skills are best left to the trained performer.

The Kamikaze! Downhill

When the Kamikaze! was first held, no one was sure what the outcome would be. Would the course be littered with bruised bodies and bloody bikes? Would the winners be deranged thrill seekers with a death wish? As it turned out, relatively few accidents occurred in comparison to other bicycle races. Those who wanted to just complete the course held their speed down, and those who wanted to win let it all hang out.

Jim Deaton, a pro rider, was the winner. Considered the best downhiller of his day, his skill and attitude got him down the course safely. Behind him were two local boys who worked at the ski lift, and practiced the downhill daily after work.

You get to the top of the course on an aerial tram, the gondola. A start ramp sits a few yards from the actual summit. You mount the ramp with your bike and get ready for the ride of your life.

"Racer ready! Get set! GO!" Down the ramp onto a wide run, you pass ski runs with names like "Hangman's Hollow" and "Wipeout." The dirt is loose, the terrain is steep and it's tough to keep your bike upright. Sit back, keep a straight line, pinch your seat in your thighs and hold on tight.

The Kamikaze! downhill is the place to go fast on your bike, not on the trails in your neighborhood. It is reckless and unforgiving. You can get killed doing this. Be sure that you have as much protective clothing on as possible, including a helmet. You can practice for this kind of event on an isolated road that you know is free of traffic. If you are going to commit hari- kari, just be sure that you don't take anyone along with you.

Competition brings together all the skills of mountain biking in a fun and exciting way. The wonderful thing about competition is that nobody takes it too seriously, and everyone is willing to help each other out. I was racing in the World Championships in the cross-country event. As the pack of racers began to string out on the narrow road, it became difficult to pass. Instead of slower racers holding their ground, refusing to let others pass, there was a co-operation among the racers. One racer would say to me, "Boy, you are looking a lot stronger than me, go ahead and pass me." Or "Excuse me, do you mind if I pass you up here on this wider section?" This amicable attitude is what makes mountain bike racing so much fun. Everyone is out there to just be on the bike and have a good time.

9. MOUNTAIN BIKE MAINTENANCE

Maintaining your mountain bike is easy and anyone can do it. Knowing how your bike works can save you money and a long walk out of the woods.

Invest in your own set of basic tools, if you are interested in maintaining your bike on a regular basis. Here is a list of tools that every home mechanic should have. Check at a bike shop for pre-assembled tool kits or for some of these specialized bicycle tools.

1. Metric wrenches
    a. Open end type — sizes 17, 16, 15, 14, 10, 9, 8 mm
    b. Allen wrenches — sizes 6, 5, 4 mm
2. Chain rivet tool
3. Small slothead screwdriver
4. Tire levers
5. Pair of standard pliers
6. Tube patch kit
    With a set like this you can do all necessary basic repairs.

Keep It Clean

The first rule of bicycle maintenance is keep it clean. A dirty bike is an unhealthy bike. Mountain bikes get especially dirty and demand special attention. After a dirty ride, wipe your bike down with a damp cloth. If the dirt or mud is thick DO NOT take your bike to the local car wash for the high pressure hose. A dousing like this could remove the grease from your bearings and freeze up the internal parts. If you have to use a hose, avoid spraying directly at the areas where bearings are located and use a very low pressure stream of water. Chains should be periodically removed and cleaned in a solvent. (see "Chain Repair" to remove and replace chain.) Relubricate your chain with a Teflon or silicone-based lubricant. Be sure to wipe off excess lubricant.

Fixing A Flat

Some fools pay bike shops to do this basic repair. However, there isn't always a bike shop located just around the bend. Part of mountain biking is the ability to make-in-the field repairs. Fixing a flat is not that difficult. Mountain bike racers must replace a tube and be back on the road as quick as possible; often in less than five minutes.

If you hear that hissing sound on your ride or feel that flop-flop-flop below, stop immediately to avoid damage to your tire or wheel. Damage can occur when the rim hits a hard object like a rock or curb. The tire can become shredded and thus unrepairable as it gets crushed between the rim and the road.

To repair a flat, remove the wheel. Close your brake pads against the rim with one hand and release the straddle cable from the non-fixed side of the brake with your other hand. Now let go of the brakes and remove the wheel. If you have a quick release style hub (with a lever that flips outwards), open the lever to loosen the wheel and remove the wheel from your frame. If you have a bolted style hub (one with lug nuts) use a wrench to loosen the nuts and remove the wheel. Removing the rear wheel is a little trickier than the front wheel. While standing behind the bicycle, reach down and gently pull the rear derailleur back toward you. Then push the wheel forward and down to clear the chain.

Once the wheel is removed, pull out your tire irons. Push the dished end of the irons between the tire and the rim and pry one side of the tire up and over the rim. Some irons will have a hook on the opposite end so you can hang it on a spoke and keep your hands free while you work with a second iron. Take the second iron and pry the other side of the tire off the rim. If you are unable to remove one side of the tire from the rim with just two levers, you may have to repeat the process with a third tire iron. Yet, the wide mountain bike tire usually comes off quite easily.

Pull the tube out of the tire while leaving the valve stem attached to the rim. Grab your bike pump and fill the tube with air until you find the hole. Now replace the tube in the tire to find where the corresponding puncture hole is in the tire. Look for a thorn, piece of glass or any other object that may have punctured

Figure 23

Fixing a flat tire.

A)   Pinch tire from the side to remove tire.

B)   Pump tire up to find leak.

C)   Fix tire using tire wrenches.

D)   Tire patch.

A

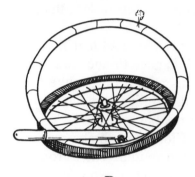

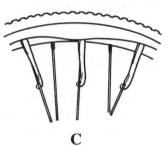

C   **D**

B

your tube. Remove it. Run your hand carefully around the inside of the tire feeling for any other possible puncture- makers.

If it is a small hole, mark it and grab your patch kit. Inside you'll find an abrasive pad, patches, and a tube of glue. Use the abrasive pad to lightly roughen the surface of the tube. This creates a better bond between patch and tube. Apply a thin layer of glue to the area around the hole making it slightly larger than the patch itself. Allow it to dry for several minutes.

Notice that your patch has a plastic side and a foil side. Peel the foil side off the patch taking care not to touch the exposed area. Center it over the hole with your fingers. Apply pressure to the center of the patch and work out toward the edges. Use the curved edge of a tire iron to apply pressure to the area. Gently peel back the plastic off the top of the patch taking care not to peel up the edges of the patch off the tube.

Install the valve stem in the rim and work the tube back into the tire, working in opposite directions, ending across the wheel from the valve stem. Now put one side of the tire back in the rim. Start at the valve stem again and use your tire levers to work the tire back onto the rim. You will encounter more resistance as you try to work in the last bit of tire. Be careful not to pinch the tube between your rim and the lever or it may get punctured again. Also, be sure that your valve is straight. A crooked valve may break.

As you pump up the tire, watch the edge of the rim. Make sure your tube is not bubbling out from between tire and rim. If this happens, immediately deflate the tire at the valve, gently tuck the tube inside the tire, and reinflate.

Put your wheel back on. Make sure your wheel is properly secured on the bike with the quick release or axle nuts. Don't forget to re-fasten and check your brakes.

Patching a tire is an inexpensive way to fix a flat. But patches can develop slow leaks that will take you by surprise when you are too far from home. I usually just buy another tube whenever I develop a flat. It feels secure knowing that you won't have to pump up your tire every fifteen minutes. Always carry an extra tube and a patch kit whenever you go for a ride.

Truing Your Wheel

When your wheel wobbles or bumps against your brake pads while you're riding, chances are you need to have your wheel trued. Wheel truing is a technique that tightens or loosens spokes to make the wheel round and true. To determine if your wheel needs truing, hold a pencil about a 1/8" from the rim and spin it. If the pencil touches the rim, or if you squeeze your spokes two at a time and find they feel loose or spongy, you probably should have your wheel trued. This is a technique beyond the scope of this book. If you really think your wheel needs truing, see your local bike mechanic.

Adjusting Brakes

Brakes are important. They will save your life. You should know how to adjust them at home and on a ride. Your brakes need attention when you notice one or more of the following:

a) they make an awful squealing noise
b) when you apply your brakes nothing happens
c) you have a pad rubbing constantly on the rim
d) your brake pads are in contact with your tire (instead of the rim).

Most mountain bikes today have cantilever brakes (see illust-ration) and the techniques outlined below are written assuming this is your brake design. If you have U-brakes or rollercam brakes, consult your local bike shop for details on repair or adjustment.

Even if your brakes are not causing any of the problems men-tioned above, they still need to be adjusted on occasion. First look at where your brake pads come in contact with the rim. The brake pad should be centered on the rim without rubbing the tire. If it is not centered, take an allen wrench (5 or 6 mm) and insert it in the bolt that holds the pad stud. Now, take a 10 mm open-end wrench and loosen the nut on the opposite side of the bolt. This will allow you to maneuver the pad until it lines up with the rim correctly. While performing this adjustment, you want to make sure that the

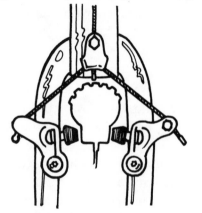

Figure 24
Proper bake pad alignment.

front of the pad (the side that is towards the front of the bike) contacts the rim before the back of the pad does. This should be approximately 1/16" to 1/8" from the rim. This prevents the brakes from squealing.

To tighten the brakes, you want to remove the slack from your brake cables. Before you do this, you must turn the adjusting barrel on your brake lever. Turn the barrel clockwise until you have approximately 4 mm of threads showing. This will enable you to fine-tune the brakes once the cable is tightened.

Now, compress the brake pads tightly to the rim (with the help of a friend or by tying the pads in place). Then loosen the cable binder bolt located at the end of the cable. Pull the cable firmly down with a pair of pliers. Tighten the binder bolt while holding the cable in place.

Now give the brake lever a couple of good solid squeezes and then spin the wheel to be sure that the pads are centered and not rubbing on the rim. If they are too close, turn the adjusting barrel on the brake lever clockwise until you have enough clearance on the rim. If the pads are rubbing on one side or the other, slide your cable carrier to the left or right. Squeeze the lever again and recheck your adjustment. In a pinch, you can use the adjusting barrel to tighten your brakes. But, don't rely on this adjustment exclusively. It is best to tighten the cable, and use the barrel for fine-tuning.

Adjusting Gears

When you shift your gears you move a lever that pulls a cable. This cable moves your derailleurs. The derailleur moves your chain over the appropriate gear. The chain is prevented from going too far in either direction by properly adjusted derailleur stops.

An improperly adjusted derailleur causes over-shifting (when your chain shifts off the cogs or chain ring); under-shifting (when your chain won't shift into the next gear) or automatic shifting (when you haven't even touched the lever). A properly adjusted derailleur hits all your gears quietly, quickly, and precisely while you pedal.

To adjust your derailleur, it helps to have a bike stand to get your bike off the ground. If you don't have access to one, you can hang your bike by its seat and handlebars. First, pull the right hand thumbshifter all the way back towards you while cranking the pedal forward. The chain should be on the smallest cog in the rear. If it's gone past and over shifted between the cog and frame, you need to set your outside derailleur stop. This is done by tightening a screw marked "H" (for high gear) on the derailleur. Carefully lift the chain back on to the smallest cog. Then, turn the "H" screw clockwise with a small slothead screwdriver until you meet resistance. Do not overtighten. If you are under-shifting and not reaching the small cog, you need to loosen (turn counter-clockwise) the "H" screw until the chain engages on the cog.

While you have the chain on the small cog, check your cable tension. Loosen the bolt that holds the cable to the rear derailleur.

Grasping the end of the cable with a pair of pliers, gently pull the excess cable slack and retighten the binder bolt.

Now check the low gear stop on the rear derailleur. While cranking the pedal again, push the right hand thumbshifter away from you. If your chain shifts between the cog and your spokes, pull the lever slightly back until the chain is engaged squarely on the largest cog. Now turn the screw marked "L" (for low) in clockwise manner until you meet resistance. Do not overtighten. At this point your rear derailleur should be properly adjusted. Check the adjustment by cranking your pedal forward and running through the gears by moving your shift lever forward and back. If the

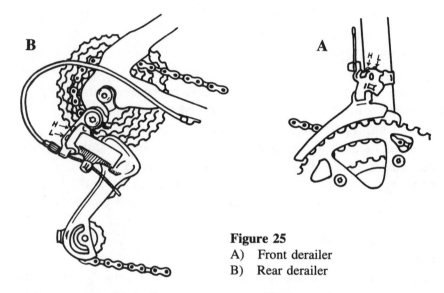

Figure 25
A)   Front derailer
B)   Rear derailer

derailleur hesitates or still over or under-shifts, readjust the appropriate stop screw.

If you have an indexed shift system, it is not much different to adjust than a friction system. Have your local bike mechanic show you how to fine tune it. With an index system you should have a switch on your right hand thumbshifter that allows you to change into a standard friction system. Check to see how your shifter changes from one mode to the other because they are not all the same. If your index system isn't working when you're out in the middle of nowhere, you can switch to the friction system until you can get it adjusted.

Adjusting the front derailleur is the same as adjusting the rear derailleur, however, there are a couple of things you need to check. With your left hand thumbshifter pulled all the way toward you and while cranking the pedal forward, look down at your chain. It should be on the smallest chain ring. If it isn't, turn the left hand screw or the screw marked "L" on your front derailleur counter-clockwise. At the same time slowly crank the pedal forward until the chain drops onto the small chain ring. Look directly over the front derailleur and check to make sure that the right hand edge of the derailleur cage is parallel with the chain rings. If it's not, loosen the bolt that holds the derailleur onto the frame and rotate the derailleur (without allowing it to drop) into a position parallel with the chain ring and tighten the bolt.

Now take the slack out of the cable. Loosen the cable binder bolt and grasp the cable with a pair of pliers, gently pulling the cable until snug. Retighten the bolt while holding the cable in place. To set the high gear stop on the front derailleur, push the left hand thumbshifter away from you while cranking the pedal. If the chain falls off the outside of the large chain ring, gently hand place the chain on the larger chain ring and pull the thumbshifter slightly back so the front derailleur is centered over the chain. Now take your small slothead screwdriver and turn the "H" or right hand screw until you meet resistance. Do not overtighten. Now shift through your front gears to make sure the derailleur is not over-or under-shifting.

Chain Removal And Repair

Often it is necessary to remove your chain for periodic cleaning or to replace it. To remove the chain, take your chain rivet tool and place your chain within the front guides (farthest from the t-handle). Slowly rotate the t-handle in a clockwise manner making sure that the pin attached to the handle is pushing directly against the side of pin connecting the two chain links in the guides. Without completely removing the chain pin from the links, push it out until the far end is flush with the outside edge of the tool. Turn the t-handle counter-clockwise to back it out of the links. Remove the tool from the chain and gently snap the links apart. One of the links should still contain the pin. If the pin is not in either link, you will need to take the chain to a bike shop.

After you clean the chain, put it back together by reversing the link positions in the chain tool guide. Push the pin back into the links with the t-handle. With the chain back on the bike, slowly crank the pedal backwards and watch the chain run through the rear derailleur cage. It should run smooth and quiet. If it hops or has stiff links, determine which links are stiff by flexing the links with your hands. Grab your chain tool and set the stiff links across

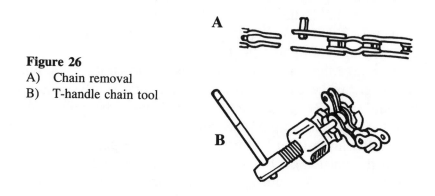

Figure 26
A)   Chain removal
B)   T-handle chain tool

the set of guides closest to the t-handle. Turn the t-handle clockwise until it touches the pin in the links and give it approximately 1/4 turn more. CAUTION: Do not turn the t-handle too far. Turn it only enough to loosen the link, not to take it apart. Do this with each stiff link and then recheck that the chain moves smoothly and quietly while cranking the pedal backwards. When you're finished relubricate your chain.

Now you've got the basics. With a little practice and a little patience you should be able to keep your gears and brakes fine tuned, your tires inflated, and your chain running smoothly. If you have questions or problems with your adjustments and repairs, don't hesitate to see your local bike mechanic and get your bike checked by a pro.

10. THE MOUNTAIN BIKE
AS A TEACHER

From my vantage point atop my bike, the world lies beneath me. I have climbed to this point in less than an hour; an ascent that would take three hours on foot. The trail winds back down the moraine, into the glacial valley below. This machine can glide me through the forested slopes safely, forever descending towards home.

However, I choose to challenge myself. The descent will be my fastest. Staying in control, I will push myself to make the descent in record time. Along the way, I will not stop for boulders and logs. Every obstacle will be cleared, and my foot will never dab the forest floor. I realize there are risks in my course action and prepare for them accordingly.

I pull a pair of knee pads from my pack, slip jeans over my shorts and buckle my helmet. I pause and visualize the trail I have just ascended. On the open stretches I will be swift, at each hindrance, caution is essential. Obstacles that I have tried a hundred times become fresh in my mind once again. Attitude is important. It will keep me upright and alive.

I apply one stroke of power to the pedals and let gravity do the work. The trail is rocky. I sit upright and absorb the shock with my legs. A switchback. I brake, balance on my stationary bike, turn the wheel sharply, and slowly creep around the curve. A straight-a-way. The chain wraps around the largest gear, and I am off. I scan the terrain, programming each variation, responding with deliberation. I hold my line straight through the sand, pull a wheelie across a water bar. I am exhilarated — but careful.

I imagine a competition that requires these skills. A race where control is as important as speed. A course with obstacles is laid out. Between obstacles the riders run rapid. At each barrier care is taken. Racers are judged on time and ability. The race mimics the sport of mountain biking, closer than any event I can think of. And I am its first competitor.

I slow down for the boulders. I conceive my line. Front tire weaves through the first rocks; rear tire rides over them. Pull up on the front wheel for the large boulder, turning slightly to set up my rear tire for the descent. As my thought finishes, I am into the rocks. I feel my rear tire slam over them as I prepare for the big boulder. Front wheel up, stand up and turn slightly, lean towards the ...

Figure 27
Sometimes crashing is inevitable.

I am falling. My body leaps over the handlebars towards the brush. The bike crashes atop me as I struggle to get out of its way. I don't react in time and find myself pinned.

Through some freak of topology, I am caught between the handlebars and the top tube. My body lays across the bike and the wheel, preventing extraction. My heartbeat slows, the sounds of the forest creep in, and I pause, wondering how I am to get out of here.

Fortunately, I am not hurt. But I am stuck. I think of self-sufficiency. There comes a time in mountain biking where you feel prepared and realize you are not. All I need is another hand to lift the jammed handlebars from my legs, and I can finish this ride. I swear to never go alone on a ride to a remote area. Yet, it doesn't help my current predicament.

With agonizing slowness, I inch my arms under the bike and extricate myself from this trap. I cannot believe this has happened. What if it is a broken leg? I am lucky.

Although self-sufficiency and control are imperative in mountain biking, there are times when you need to humble yourself. You may be the best downhiller in the world, but you are not infallible. No matter how well you've prepared, or how many skills you have acquired, you can go over the handlebars for the last time. Watch it. Be aware. Have fun.

* * * *

Back on the bike. I hit the final turns of the descent. They are wide and predictable. I fly around each one in a controlled skid. I was disqualified in my imaginary race. Now I can relax and enjoy the ultimate ending to a wonderful ride.

As I creep up to my car, I look back at my mountain. The setting sun ignites its piney carpet in deep red. Across the meadow, a family of deer graze peacefully. I wipe the sweat from my face, and gaze at my bike. "You are a feisty one," I say to its dusty frame, "but you sure do know how to show me a good time."

GLOSSARY & INDEX

Adjusting Barrel: (58-59) Fine-tune tension adjustment on brake lever.

Allen Wrench: (19, 58) Hexagonal wrench.

ATB: (40) All Terrain Bicycle.

Beginner: (48, 50) A racer who has never raced before.

Bike Stand: (59) Apparatus that lifts bike off-the ground to repair wheel.

Binder Bolt: (58, 60) Bolt that holds tension on brake cable adjustments.

Bottom Bracket: (38) The bearings and axle of the pedal system.

BMX: (5, 10, 16, 51) Bicycle Moto-Cross; the first bikes to be ridden in the dirt.

Butt-bag: (19) A pack carried around the waist.

Cable Lock: (21) A bike lock consisting of a braided cable: can be cut with bolt cutters.

Cadence: (23) Pedaling rhythm.

Cantalever Brakes: (58) Brake system that pulls both pads simultaneously.

Chain ring: (3, 16, 33-34, 36, 38, 59) Cog or gear on pedal side of gear system.

Chain Rivet Tool: (19, 54, 61) Tool for removal of the master link in a chain.

Clean: (54) To complete an observed trials section without a dab.

Cog: (59-60) Gear.

Crank: (37) Stem that attaches pedal to the chain ring.

Cross-bike: (5-6) A hybrid bike that utilized both mountain and road bike design.

Cruiser: (5) A low priced bike that has similar characteristics as a mountain bike.

Dab: (14, 51) To touch your feet to the ground during an observed trials.

Derailluer: (27, 55, 60-62) Mechanism that shifts the chain between gears.

Double Track: (44) A dirt road.

Down Tube: (19) Tube on bike frame that runs from the fork to the bottom bracket.

Freestyle: (16, 51) A type of biking where tricks and stunts are performed.

Gears: (16-17, 23, 37, 62) Cogs.

Head Tube: Tube on bike frame that runs from the fork to the bottom bracket.

Hopping: (34-35, 15-16) Trials technique where bike is hopped up and over obstacles.

Hybrid Bike: (6) See Cross-bike.

Hydro Plane: (38) the ability of the bike to skim over water without touching the ground.

Hyper-glide: (17) Dishes in cogs that allow smoother shifting under load.

Intermediate: (48) Racing classification; have raced 5 races.

Kamikaze: (11, 52-53) A downhill competition held at Mammoth Mountain, CA.

Masters: (48) Racing classification; Age 45 and up.

Modified Bike: (48, 51-52) Racing classification for Trials; a bike that has been designed for observed trials competition.

Mountain Bike: (9) A bike designed for riding off-road.

Mountain Touring Bike: (8) Mountain bike with modifications for carrying loads.

NORBA: (40-41) National Off-Road Bicycle Assn.; Oversees mountain bike racing and access.

Observed Trials: (51) Competition where riders negotiate obstacles.

Obstacle: (3, 12, 32-39, 63-64) Any rock, boulder, log, stairs, curb, puddle, etc.

Pannier: (19) Bike pack that mounts on the side of the bike.

Racing Bike: (5, 10) Mountain bike designed for competition; usually lighter than stock bike.

Rim: (1, 55-56) Part of wheel that holds tire in place.

Roller Cam Brake: (58) Brakes that utilize cams to increase tension.

Saddlebag: (19) Pack that hangs under the seat.

Seat Tube: (26) Tube on frame that connects seat to bottom bracket.

Section: (51) A complete obstacle in Trials.

Single Speed: (48) Racing classification for one speed bikes.

Single Track: (41-42, 49) A narrow path or trail.

Skid Turn: (13-14) A turn where the rider skids the rear wheel without stopping.

Slickrock: (44-45) Geologic formation consisting of slippery rock.

Spin: (23) See cadence.

Stock Bike: (48, 51) Racing classification for trails; normal mountain bike as sold to the public.

Super: (48) Racing classification; top level amateurs.

Switchback: (42-43, 63) Where a trail or road that traverses a slope switches directions.

T-Handle: (61-62) Part of chain tool that removes the pin in the master link by rotating it.

Thumbshifter: (59-61) Shift levers mounted on handlebars.

Tire Iron: (19, 55) Long tool with a hook on one end and a shallow dish on the other end for removing the tire from the rim.

Toe Clip: (14-15, 19, 24) Basket or clamp that holds the foot onto the Pedal.

Topographic Map: (21) Map that shows geographic feature as well as roads.

Top Tube: (19) Tube that connects seat tube to the head tube.

Trials Bike: (5, 7, 16, 51) Bike designed for observed trials competition.

True: (57) Process of adjusting spokes to reduce wobble in the rim of a wheel.

U-Lock: (21) Heavy duty lock that cannot be cut with bolt cutters.

Vet: (48) Racing classification; ages 35-45.

Wheelie: (15, 33, 35, 46) Technique where front wheel is pulled off the ground.

the Outdoors

Each only $4.95

The Basic Essentials Series

Backpacking
Harry Roberts
ISBN 0-934802-44-0

First Aid For The Outdoors
Dr. William Forgey
ISBN 0-934802-43-2

Map & Compass
Cliff Jacobsen
ISBN 0-934802-42-4

Edible Wild Plants and Useful Herbs
Jim Meuninch
ISBN 0-934802-41-6

Canoeing
Cliff Jacobsen
ISBN 0-934802-39-4

Camping
Cliff Jacobsen
ISBN 0-934802-38-6

ICS BOOKS, Inc.

Ask for any of these titles at your favorite outdoor equipment outlet or bookstore.
For a complete catalog of ICS Book titles for outdoor lifestyles call 1-800-541-7323.